Text and photographs copyright © 1995 David Boag
This edition copyright © 1995 Lion Publishing

The author asserts the moral right
to be identified as the author of this work

Published by
Lion Publishing plc
Sandy Lane West, Oxford, England
ISBN 0 7459 3306 8
Albatross Books Pty Ltd
PO Box 320, Sutherland, NSW 2232, Australia
ISBN 0 7324 1259 5

First edition 1995

10 9 8 7 6 5 4 3 2 1 0

A catalogue record for this book is available
from the British Library

Printed and bound in Malaysia

Birds of the Air

Look at the birds of the air; they do not sow and reap and store in barns, yet your heavenly father feeds them.

DAVID BOAG

A LION BOOK

Introduction

I must have been a very difficult child. My earliest recollections are of sitting on a rug in front of the fire playing with dozens of little plastic animals. Squares on the lino became fields, the rug became a huge wood and an old table cloth draped over cushions became mountains and valleys. Even at that early age I can remember that I would not mix kangaroos with lions, for they live a continent apart in the wild. Neither would I mix foxes with rabbits, for more obvious reasons, unless I felt the fox was hungry – I was never sentimental about the natural world.

It was not long before plastic animals lost their fascination and I discovered the real thing in our suburban garden. Most creatures were quite small and harmless: woodlice, centipedes, ladybirds and caterpillars now roamed my make-believe world. But I longed to own more.

Looking back, my parents must have been true saints for I can remember few objections when I hatched about 200 peacock butterflies in my bedroom. When released, the gardens around were decorated with them for weeks. I think it was this incident which inspired my parents to give me a range of old chicken sheds as a play room and I promptly began breeding mice and rabbits. My collection rapidly grew – frogs, toads and newts were popular and easy to get from a pond about two miles away. A grass snake was my pride and joy until one day I caught an injured jay. On rainy days I would sneak the jay indoors and, sitting it on my pillow, would release a spider at the foot of the bed. The jay would move like lightning to catch its prey.

I never quite lost the desire to collect the things I discovered in the natural world so I bought a second-hand camera to capture them on film. Today I thank God that I can share in the things he created by spending my time as a professional wildlife photographer. I not only discover constant pleasure in the natural environment, but I also enjoy the responsibility of caring for and protecting the things he has created.

Many of the Psalms in the Bible contain wonderful images of the natural world and the glory of God. One day I came upon the words 'gaze upon the beauty of the Lord'. That's impossible I thought; you can't see God, so how can you gaze upon his beauty? For a while I sat quietly thinking and at last in frustration I said out loud, 'How can I see your beauty?' Into my mind came images of many of the wonderful places I had visited which were special to me.

I pictured myself walking along a lonely coast path looking down on the sea as the sun made it sparkle like a jewel. My thoughts went to the Scottish Highlands where, after a hard climb, I was rewarded with the beauty and majesty of miles of rugged countryside. I remembered a loch and an otter gently twisting and turning in the water a few yards away from me. And, as I thought of the kingfisher I had held in my hand and the seed head of goat's-beard I had picked, I knew I had seen God's beauty.

God's creation reflects his character and I have been fortunate enough to gaze upon some of the most beautiful things he has created. I hope that in the pages of this book I can share with you some of the beauty I have discovered.

Jay

In my youth I found a jay that could not fly. It was a fledgling but all of the main flight feathers on its left wing were missing, and all it could do was to flutter in circles. After some effort I captured it and put it in the saddle-bag of my bicycle. Eagerly, I took it home, and installed my prize in a large aviary.

I would spend hours talking to the jay through the wire of its prison. Sometimes, just when it seemed most interested in my conversation, it would dash across the cage and snatch a spider: obviously I didn't have its full attention at all!

I became very fond of my jay and it would follow me around the garden, hopping rapidly across the lawn if I got too far away. Together we made for the rockery and the jay would sit on a boulder, with its head cocked to one side as I heaved up a great rock. Underneath dashed the jay, diligently searching out every insect and worm before returning to its perch, calling for me to lift another rock.

One day I got too far away for comfort and to my astonishment it flew the length of the garden with complete mastery of the air. I wondered how long it had been able to fly. We continued to be friends for many more months and played all the old games even though it could fly. In a way I became even more fond of it, because it could easily have left me if it wanted to.

This is similar to my relationship with God: I have complete freedom to come or go when I choose. But I trust and believe that his greatest pleasure comes when I choose to remain close to his side.

Blue Tit

B lue tits must surely be one of the most popular and easily recognizable garden birds. Their antics keep us constantly entertained as they investigate every nook and cranny for insects in the trees and shrubs. They also feed readily on peanuts suspended in a wire container, or on coconut halves hung from the branch of a tree. Indeed it is not difficult to get them feeding within a few inches of the kitchen window.

It would seem, therefore, that they would be easy to photograph, but the problem is that they are always on the move. One moment a blue tit is perched upside-down on the peanuts; the next, with a quick flick of its wings, it's on the honeysuckle. Driven to distraction on more than one occasion, I have begged a blue tit just to be still for a second, while I take its picture.

I am certain that there are occasions when, for more profound reasons, God begs us to be still for a moment. There's a story in the Bible which tells of two sisters, Mary and Martha. Jesus shared a meal with them. One of the sisters, Martha, busied herself preparing the meal; but it was Mary he commended for sitting down and listening to all he said. Often we become so busy doing good things that it becomes impossible for us to open ourselves up to God.

Buzzard

Snuggled together in the bottom of the nest, four fluffy buzzard chicks wait patiently for their parents to return. At this stage they look so vulnerable, relying totally on their parents for food, protection and shelter from the rain. They remain in the nest for six or seven weeks, but in the final fortnight they become more independent. They are larger, and with their feathers developed they no longer need protection and shelter.

When the buzzard chicks fly, they are fully grown; but until they become proficient hunters they still need to be fed by their parents. There comes a time, however, when the young birds must leave, and the adults encourage them to fend for themselves.

Those of us who are parents know how it feels when our youngsters grow up. As our sons and daughters mature we find they don't rely on us so much and have their own ideas. Sometimes it's hard to let them go.

I can remember a conscious decision I made when my son was in his mid-teens. I felt it was time I began to change our relationship from father to friend. It was not easy at first but, looking back, it was a good decision. My son is now my best friend; oddly enough, I feel more of a father to him than I did before.

When a buzzard leaves the nest it becomes an adversary or a competitor to its parents, because buzzards are territorial. I am so glad that this doesn't have to be true of our relationships with our children.

Chaffinch

Hidden among the prickly stems of a bramble bush, I found the nest of a chaffinch. The bird was not present, but I still knew who owned the nest simply by the way it was made. This brought many questions to my mind. How does a chaffinch know it has to make its nest out of moss, and not out of small twigs or dead grass as some other birds do? What makes the chaffinch want to begin to build the nest in the first place? How does it know where to start? Does it know what is going on when it is about to lay its eggs, and then how does it know to lay them in the nest? Until now it has only fed itself, so why does it feed the little scraps that hatch from the eggs (after all it has probably never had baby chicks before)?

Of course, the answer to all these questions is that all creatures have 'a fixed pattern of behaviour in response to certain stimuli'. That is the dictionary definition of 'instinct'. How many wonders of nature do we simply sweep aside with that word 'instinct'! Each time I use that word, I stop for a moment to consider the miracle of creation.

Cormorant

'Jizz' is a word used by ornithologists to describe the overall impression that a bird gives, and it is this impression that enables an experienced bird-watcher to identify the species. Once, on a bitterly cold winter's morning, I was crouched down watching a cormorant. My steamy breath hung on the air and I pulled my jacket tighter around me. Even with my binoculars I could not see any detail in the plumage as I peered through swirling mist, but I knew it was a cormorant. Its size, shape, the way it behaved – in other words its jizz – all added up to a cormorant.

The word was invented by a Cheshire ornithologist many years ago and, like other jargon, it became part of the bird-watcher's vocabulary.

Sometimes it is impossible to find words to express ourselves adequately, but at least I know that when I'm speaking to God he knows exactly what I mean, even if words fail me.

Great Spotted Woodpecker

I magine being faced with the towering trunk of a tree and being told you had to make a hole in it, large enough to accommodate yourself and a growing family. This is the challenge that a woodpecker faces at the beginning of each breeding season. If it were our task, it would help greatly to have a chain saw. The woodpecker is equally well-equipped for the job it faces.

Watching the bird hammering at a tree it seems a miracle that its physique can withstand such violent blows. The woodpecker, however, has a specially designed upper jaw, or mandible. Muscles that operate the beak and a layer of shock-absorbing material also provide an effective cushion, which prevents the bird knocking itself out or at least giving itself a permanent headache!

Woodpeckers also chisel out wood-boring insects with a tongue that can reach five centimetres into an insect's tunnel. The tongue is both sharp and barbed and, because it is so long, it can be withdrawn into the skull.

What an amazing piece of engineering! There is something profoundly fascinating and moving about the ingenuity and complexity of so much of the natural world. My response is to praise God for his creativity.

Canada Goose

As the name suggests, the Canada goose originated in North America; it was introduced to Europe to ornament the lakes of country houses. However, the species quickly spread into the wild and is commonly found today in a variety of fresh water habitats. These birds can migrate long distances and, although even longer journeys are made by smaller birds, migrating geese seem by far the most sensational when a great skein in V-formation beats past overhead.

The reason for flying in a V-formation is that the leading bird takes much of the pressure as it flies. All the following geese are flying in the slip-stream of the bird in front, giving them an easier flight. At first this seems unfair for the leading bird, and sometimes the skein seems to collapse. It soon reforms, however, but this time with a fresh leading bird. On a long journey, many different birds may take their turn as leader.

People, too, have a responsibility to take the pressure from each other. Many of us are more than willing to hang back and let others do the work even when they seem weary. It is equally true that people who feel they are leaders don't always want to let go of the front position, even if they are wearing themselves out. Perhaps we can all learn a lesson from the geese.

Great Crested Grebe

I f I had a pound for every time a comment was made about my great enthusiasm for wildlife, I would be a rich man. The enthusiasm people see in me now, however, is nothing compared to the excited delight that I felt for nature when I was a child.

I shall never forget the first time I found a nest made by great crested grebes. I was with a friend and we had seen the grebes performing a courtship dance on the surface of the lake. They would face each other shaking their heads, or dive beneath the water to reappear with a beak-full of weed to present to each other. Several weeks later we actually found their nest hidden in the reeds. It was a mound of water vegetation and on the top were four off-white eggs.

We thought we had found a real treasure, and we were so thrilled. We both promised faithfully that we wouldn't tell a single person, not even our mothers, in case they accidentally let the secret out. We signed a scrap of paper declaring that under no circumstances would we tell about the treasure we had discovered; then we hid the paper under a stone! Over the years, of course, I have learned much about the grebe; and my enthusiasm is now complemented by knowledge.

God encourages us to remember our first love for him and to spend time learning about him so that our love will deepen. He also promises us that, no matter how we feel or what we have done, his love for us will never change.

Great Tit

One day, I was sitting in my hide watching young great tits leaving the nest. They had spent all of their short lives in the darkness of the nest, hidden in a tree cavity. The only opening to the outside world was a little hole just large enough for the parents to enter.

At last the day came for the youngsters to fledge and cautiously, each in turn, they came to the entrance. As they came from the darkness to the light, I watched them blinking as they saw the delights of the outside world for the first time. But for them to enjoy it fully, they needed to fly.

Never having tested their wings before they seemed a little uncertain. Eventually, though not fully understanding what they were doing, they trusted the air and took off. Each chick went through the same process and the last one was just as hesitant as the first; it didn't seem to help that it had watched all the others beforehand. One by one, however, they felt the air support them. They could fly! The spiritual dimension of life calls for a similar 'leap of faith'. Analysis and research can never give the whole picture – in the end we have to trust and have faith.

Grey Heron

There are some people who regard the heron as lanky, gawky and ungainly. Others consider it to be graceful and elegant. It is said that beauty is in the eye of the beholder; it is certainly true that two people may see the same bird but have completely contrasting opinions.

On one occasion I was leading a group of bird-watchers along a local river when a heron took off with huge, slow, laborious wing-beats. 'It's a fantastic bird,' a lady exclaimed, eagerly peering through her binoculars. But then she continued, 'but I hate them when they steal goldfish from my pond!' It would seem, therefore, that even the same person can have conflicting opinions, depending upon circumstances.

How often we consider that our opinion is right when perhaps there is no right or wrong – just a different way of looking at things.

Kingfisher

Some people seem to have everything going for them, and so do some birds – the kingfisher being one. It has such beautiful plumage that it has been called 'the jewel of the river' and 'the secret splendour of the brooks'. To add to its charm, it lives along the quiet rivers and streams that meander gently through the countryside. At times it dives dramatically into the water like a blue arrow, snatches a silvery fish out of the water with lightning speed. Kingfishers even nest in an interesting location: underground, in a burrow which the pair construct in the river bank.

There is another bird that seems to have little to capture the imagination: it is dull, brown and skulks about in the thickest undergrowth. But when the nightingale sings, it suddenly has something that even the kingfisher cannot equal. The kingfisher has no song, only a high-pitched whistle.

We may not be one of those people who has everything in their favour, but God looks at his children and takes pleasure in each of us. To say 'I am useless' or 'I am good for nothing' is almost an insult to God's creativity. The truth is, we are all created in his image.

Long-tailed Tit

Walking along a country path with a friend I pointed out an amazing little spherical nest in the hedge. 'That's incredible,' he exclaimed, 'what created such a beautiful and perfect nest?' I casually replied that it had just happened. 'What do you mean?' he asked.

Trying to look innocent, I explained that many years ago there had been a big bang as a farmer shot at a pigeon. He missed the bird itself, but dislodged a single feather which fluttered to the ground and became caught in the brambles. The feather then divided into two, duplicating itself. Then again and again, until there was a little bundle of tightly packed feathers in the hedge. They remained there for years, with a thick layer of moss completely surrounding them except for a little hole near the top. Spiders also found the ball and covered it with their webs, which helped to bind it all together. As the wind blew, thousands of tiny pieces of lichen stuck to the webs, decorating the nest and camouflaging it to perfection.

I had barely begun my story before my friend knew I was spinning a ridiculous yarn. As we laughed together, I suggested he used the same logic and applied it to his views on the origins of the world. If he believed that everything just happened, why didn't he believe my story?

'No, what really made it?' he insisted. 'A flying teaspoon', I replied. Then, right on cue, the long-tailed tit arrived, its tiny body and long slender tail looking just like a flying teaspoon. We moved back a few yards and were able to watch the adult bird approach the nest while the chicks poked their heads out to be fed.

Moorhen

In the early spring, when two moorhens begin to court one another they soon become inseparable. If they are out of sight of each other for more than a few minutes their loud call can be heard across the water. The bond built at this stage must last throughout the breeding season, and to help strengthen it the male will present the female with morsels of food. When the female begins incubation, she never deserts the eggs for long, so the food the male provides becomes even more crucial. Shortly after the chicks hatch, they leave the nest, following their parents wherever they go. There can be few families that stick so closely together.

Building human relationships also takes time and effort. It is important that we learn to trust each other, share with each other and enjoy each other's company. But how can this happen unless we dedicate time and care to our relationships?

Mute Swan

Walking beside a stream along a fishermen's path, my wife and I arrived at a swans' nest. I knew it was there because I had been watching it for several weeks and I knew the eggs had hatched four days previously. Although we approached carefully, however, the swans were nowhere to be seen.

In the centre of the flattened nest were two massive eggs that were cold, muddy and plainly infertile. I picked one up to show it to my wife. It completely covered the palm of her hand and weighed heavily. My wife, ever practical, exclaimed, 'If this were fresh it would feed the family for a week!' (a slight exaggeration, but it was nevertheless equal to about five or six hen's eggs). As she placed it back in the nest we joked and laughed about the best way to cook it. It was just then that the pair of swans drifted into view, followed by five of the most delightful cygnets one could imagine. Suddenly our laughter stopped: the sight of the cygnets made us realize that we were working out how to cook them!

Puffin

S itting on the top of a cliff towards the end of June, I couldn't help chuckling at the comical little puffins that surrounded me. They looked so funny as they waddled around the nest slopes, especially with their beaks full of sand-eels for their chicks hidden in the nest-burrows beneath the ground.

Puffins' clown-like appearance belies their true character, however, because they are sea birds through and through. I have been fortunate to observe them 'flying' underwater where they are incredibly fast, elegant and agile. The ocean provides everything for the puffin except, of course, a surface on which to lay their eggs – that is the only reason they ever need to come to land. They are truly masters of the ocean.

I have a friend who, whenever I meet him, is jovial and amusing, telling stories about his disastrous attempts at DIY. In the office, however, he must be a very different character, for he is very well respected and has been promoted to an extremely responsible position.

It is said that we judge a book by its cover, and perhaps we judge puffins as comic, clown-like birds because we have only seen them on the nest-slopes. How often do we judge each other when we only know part of the truth?

Reed Warbler

I n early spring a little, soberly-coloured and rather insignificant bird slips out of the reed-beds in tropical Africa and begins its migration north. It continues until it arrives in the British Isles towards the end of April. Its immediate refuge is among the reeds that flank a river or its estuary, where it disappears from view within this tall vegetation.

As its name suggests, the bird is wonderfully well-designed for life in the reeds. A slender body and short, quick wing-beats take it flicking through the reeds, hardly disturbing them at all.

Reed warblers feed on the bountiful supply of insects to be caught in the reeds, and they even create nests that are supported by the towering stems. They rely on the thick, tall vegetation for protection and cover; indeed the reeds supply all of their requirements. I don't suppose it occurs to this little bird that it could ever be otherwise.

Whenever I see a reed warbler these words from a favourite hymn come to mind:

> *All I have needed*
> *Thy hand has provided.*
> *Great is thy faithfulness*
> *Lord unto me.*

Robin

At the end of my talks people often comment that I must be very patient to photograph birds. My usual reply is, 'You should see me when I'm waiting, crouched in a hide in the freezing cold! I feel far from patient then.' But I am persistent – although mixing patience with persistence is probably better illustrated by the robin than by me.

Robins are very aggressive birds and they sing to declare their territory. They also constantly attempt to encroach on each other's property, and time and again they engage in conflict. Most of their disputes are dealt with by singing and by puffing out their red breast-feathers. In extreme circumstances, robins may even engage in a physical battle. Each time one robin approaches another's territory, it is persistently chased away; it must be a very trying problem where a large population of robins is present

As spring arrives, territories change. The robin now wants to share his territory with a mate so, sitting at a high vantage point, he sings his song even louder. For days at a time he will sing, patiently encouraging a female into his territory. The female also needs to be patient, because the male's territorial instinct is strong and she needs to adopt submissive behaviour to avoid violent rejection.

Patience and persistence go together well in prayer. I often expect God to answer prayers exactly as and when I want him to. I try to remember that God promises that he will answer, especially if I am persistent; but I sometimes need to be patient waiting for the reply.

Snipe

To most of us, the mud found on an estuary beach is little more than oozing muck that sticks to our boots and is to be avoided! The snipe, however, knows better because this mud is a rich source of food. Using its extremely long bill, it probes down into the mud where it finds a plentiful supply of worms. Indeed, during the winter, wading birds of many different species join the snipe to feed from this wealthy silt. It is said that there is more life in a cubic foot of estuary mud than a cubic foot of any other part of the land. It is full of molluscs, crustacea and worms – a vital source of food and life for countless thousands of birds.

For much of the time, the snipe searches alone, quietly getting on with its hunt for food. It keeps to the edge of the estuary, where the vegetation blends with the snipe's plumage, camouflaging its activity. Other wading birds gather in huge flocks out in the open, working together and systematically feeding on the harvest provided by the mud. It does not seem to matter how many birds are feeding, or how much they eat. There is always more life-giving goodness for them to enjoy.

I have heard the Bible described as dull, boring and of little relevance for life today. I'm sure many people are put off by its appearance and never get the chance to dig deeper to discover its riches.

Black-headed Gull

Whenever I hear the distant call of a gull, my thoughts immediately go to lazy, hot summer days – lying on a beach with my eyes closed and enjoying the heat of the sun, allowing my thoughts to wander, completely relaxed.

I am aware of a gull's presence because of its distinctive call, the call that always brings back memories of sand and sea, of childhood, of summer holidays. For some people it may bring memories of living on a farm, where gulls followed the plough. Others who have lived near the coast may have woken each morning to the gulls' plaintive cries. Their call evokes so many memories.

We all have memories, some good and some bad. Some of us have been fortunate enough to have had happy childhoods that we look back on with pleasure. Others remember their days as children with feelings of pain, anger or sorrow.

We cannot change the past, no matter how much we long to, but I have seen God heal painful memories for many people and give them fresh hope for the future. He is the God of yesterday, today and forever.

Tips for Photographing Birds

Don't spend too much time on equipment and technical know-how. Think about the more creative side of photography.

Decide what aspect about a subject particularly appeals to you. It could be the detail, the size, the atmosphere or the colour of the subject. Then you'll have a clearer idea of what it is you wish to capture, and you can attempt to exaggerate that feature.

Try to use natural light. This doesn't necessarily mean bright sunshine – some of my best photographs were taken in fog. Quite often I am forced to use flash in difficult situations, when the subject is in poor light and moving too rapidly. On these occasions, I try to reproduce natural light. I try to use only one flash, and a white card to bounce some light into the heavy-shadow areas.

Above all, use your enthusiasm, enjoying the life that surrounds you!